CARTOONS

How to Draw Cartoon Human Figures

By Jane Lindley

Table of contents

Disclaimer

While all attempts have been made to verify the information provided in this book, the author does assume any responsibility for errors, omissions, or contrary interpretations of the subject matter contained within. **The information provided in this book is for educational and entertainment purposes only. The reader is responsible for his or her own actions and the author does not accept any responsibilities for any liabilities or damages, real or perceived, resulting from the use of this information.**

The trademarks that are used are without any consent, and the publication of the trademark is without permission or backing by the trademark owner. All trademarks and brands within this book are for clarifying purposes only and are the owned by the owners themselves, not affiliated with this document.

Introduction

A lot of people today have an eye for art. The simplicity that comes from artistic work leaves a lot of people yearning for more makes them want to have an idea of how to make some of the best drawings ever.

Some of the best artists that you know today never started out as professionals. They all started from somewhere. They all built their knowledge from scratch. It is such simple drawings that spurred some of them to go on to become some of the best artistes we have ever seen in our entire lives.

It starts with a simple diagram, and then you perfect it. Having perfected some of the simple diagrams you will then be able to move on to modifications of the same. You will start working with varieties of these diagrams, better features too.

You will not only be working with the simpler diagrams, but over time you will be able to move on to drawing real life human figures. This is one of the most important ways to help you build on your knowledge and become better.

As you go on reading through this book, you will not only get information to help you work on the common figures, you will also be able to learn what to do to help you draw some of the best diagrams you have ever worked on in your life

Chapter 1: How to draw a pocketing boy

Drawing a boy is not so hard. It gets hard for a lot of people when they look at the final outcome, but in real sense you basically need to focus on the outline and you will have a good diagram done.

First you need to understand the basics. From simple art lessons, you will realize that the height of a human being is approximately 8 times the length of their head. You can take some time and measure this, play around with facts and see if it is true.

Building on that, we will use the same principle to have an outline for the body we are about to design. Draw 8 oval shapes the same size of the head of the boy you want to draw as shown below.

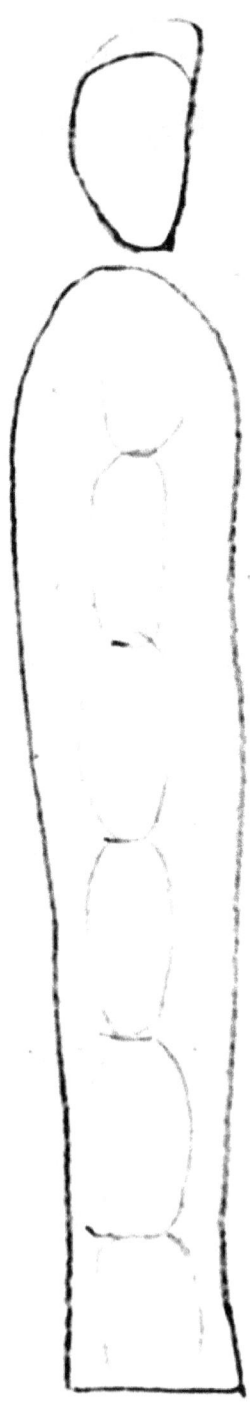

This gives us the outline of the body. Now from the oval shapes that you have already drawn, we are going to use simple lines to design the rest of the body. This should give us the frame of the body as above.

Start off from the top oval shape and use a simple line to frame the front of the man, giving you the chest and the front leg outline. Do the same for the back.

Having done that, we must also design an outline for the hair that this guy will have as sown in the diagram above.

The hairline is simple, use another simple line to design the outline.

Next up we are going to start putting some touches to the boy we are drawing, so that we can have something more distinctive.

We want to get an outline for the shirt in this step. You will use simple lines again to draw the neckline of the shirt that the boy is putting on. Having drawn the neckline, you will also need to draw an outline for the arms and the outline for the rest of the shirt as shown below.

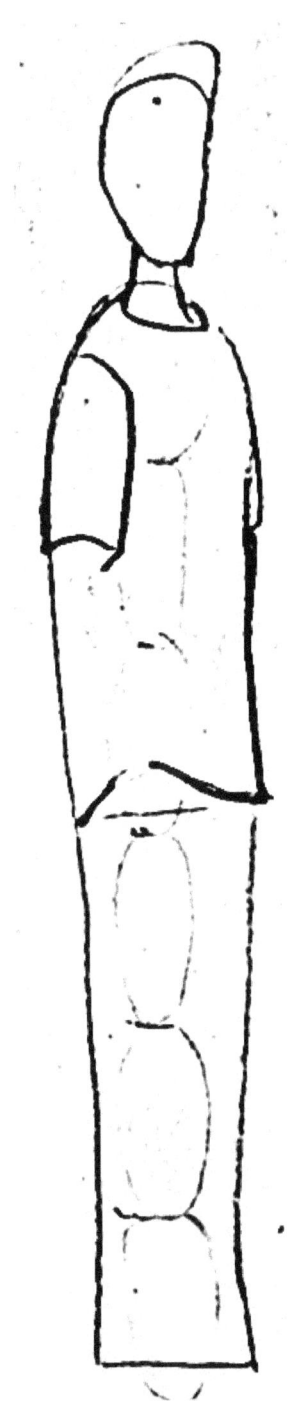

This is now getting us closer to the final diagram. You can almost see the real picture of the boy being framed right in front of your eyes.

Since we want to have him pocketing, the next idea will be to get an outline of his hands, the pocket slot on his trousers and then the shoes.

For the hands, start off a line from the shirt, drawing the outline for the elbow as you proceed.

We there are some features that should be standing out by now, such as the ears and the chin, so take time and work on those too as shown below.

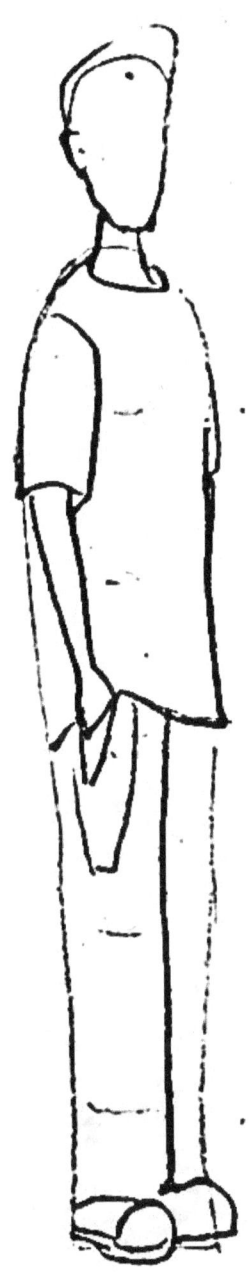

With the outline done, now we should be able to start adding the final touches to this diagram, to make it come to life.

We start off from the head and complete the hairline as shown below. For the hairline you will simply need to use some simple lines and you will be good to go. Having done that, you will then go to the other facial features such as the eyes and the nose, and the eye brows. Also use a simple line to get the shape and design of the lips.

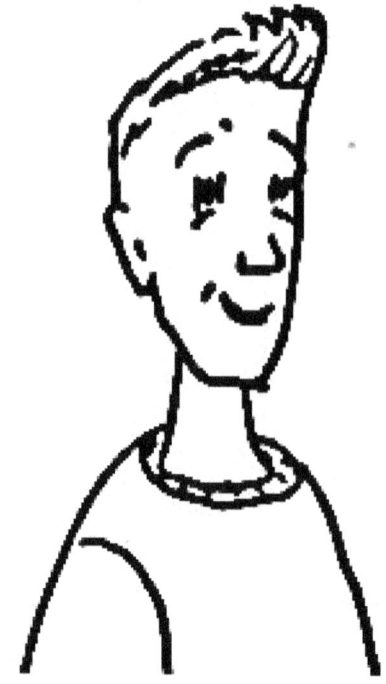

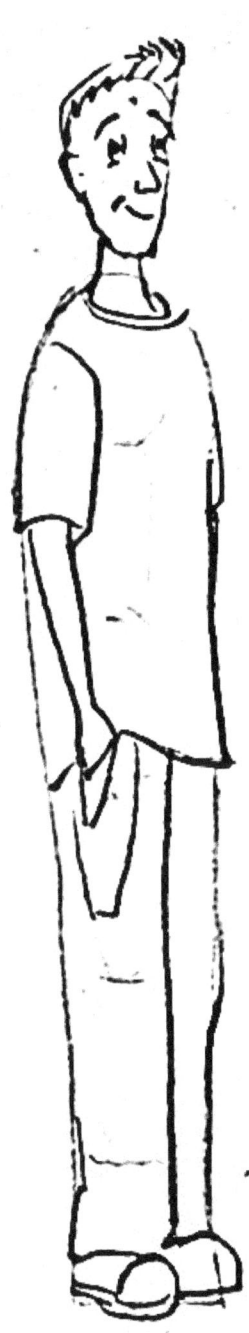

Once all that is done, you now have the outline for the boy you want. Take a darker pencil and follow through the outline of the entire body. Highlight the features that you want to stand out as shown, and then your picture will be done.

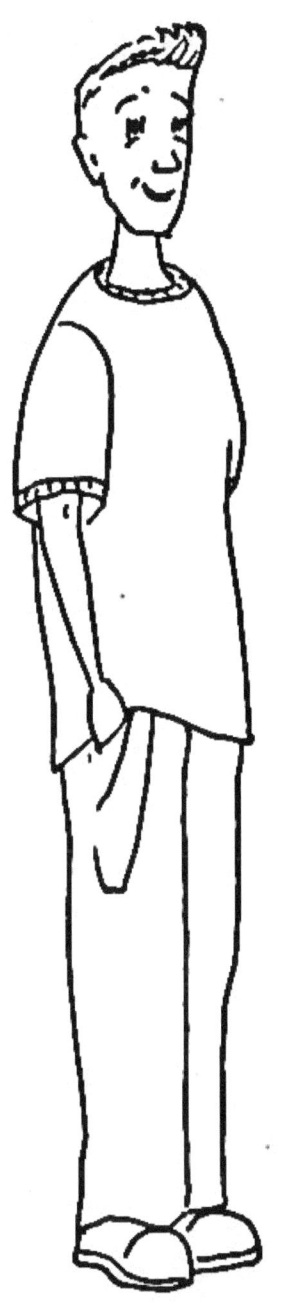

Chapter 2: Drawing a small girl

In this diagram we will be drawing a beautiful small girl. She is beautiful and happy, so we will also give her something to be happy about, her purse, awesome shoes, and a nice Mexican hat.

The first thing that we will do is to draw an outline for the hat and the dress. This will actually be one of the easiest diagrams that you can ever do so far.

The outline for the hat is simple. Draw a large oval shape. Inside the oval shape that you have drawn, proceed and draw another small oval shape. This will be the outline for the head of this small girl.

From there the outline of the dress will be drawn as shown below. The outline for the dress almost looks like a triangle, but to make it more realistic, we will curve it a bit towards the lower end.

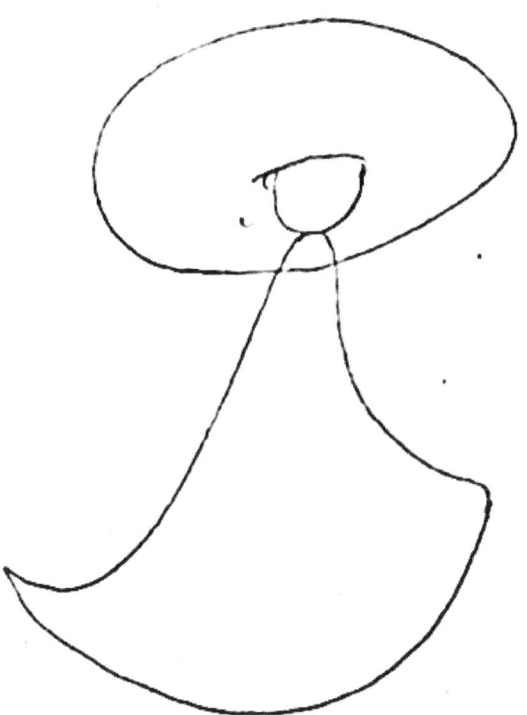

Having done that we are now going to try and draw the arms and the legs for this beautiful girl.

Drawing the arms and the legs should not be such a problem. What you need to do is to make use of simple lines that will do the trick for you.

Two lines on either side of the shoulders are supposed to work for the arms.

For the legs, you will need to use a similar pattern, flowing from the dress to the ground as shown below.

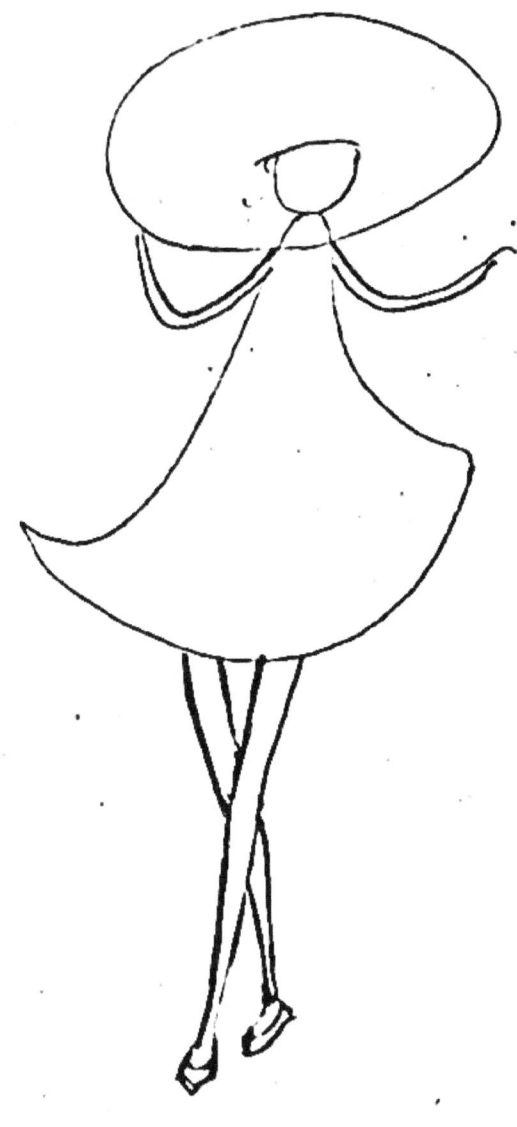

Remember to draw an outline for the shoes too.

When making these drawings, it is important for you to ensure that you do not use strong lines because you will be doing a lot of erasing. It is actually advisable for you to use a pencil that you can erase very easily.

With the outline for the rest of the body done, you can then move on to the face and try to make it stand out. The features of the face are pretty simple. You will try to draw the eyes, the nose and the lips as shown below.

Beside these features, also use small curved lines from the head to indicate an outline for her hair.

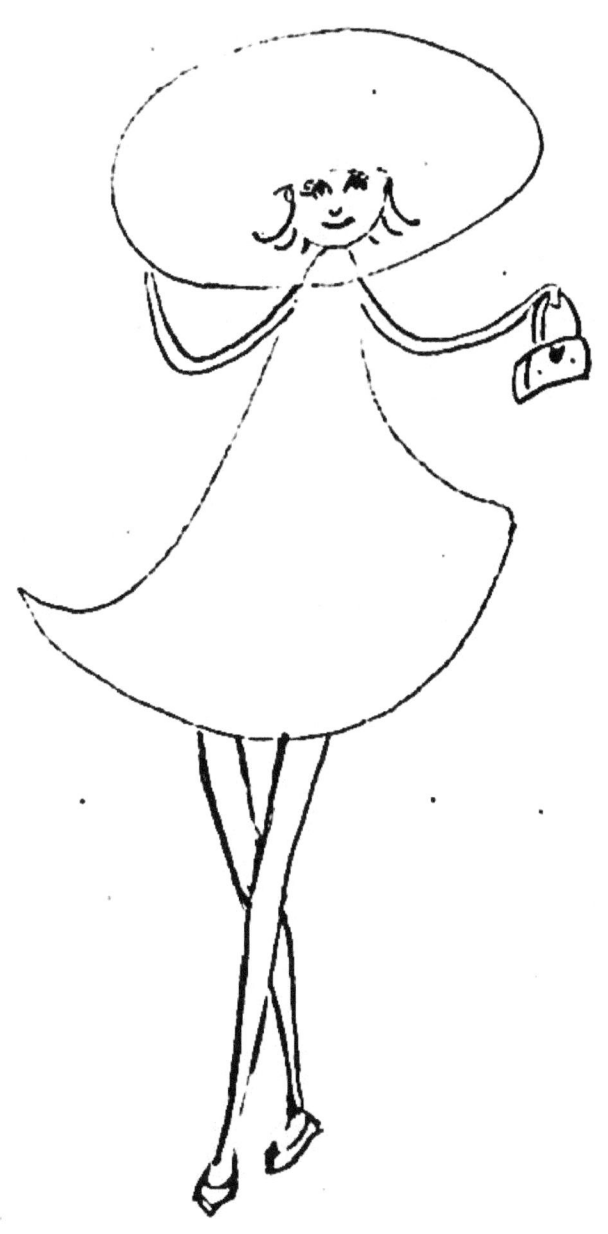

Having done that, it will now be easier for you to put on the other features such as the purse. For the purse just draw a small rectangular shape towards the end of one of her arms. Make sure you do not leave it hanging, and insert a small finger into the diagram, or her hands as you would wish, to show that she is holding the purse.

Once that is don, we can now start working on the outline for the rest of the body of this girl. This outline is for the hat and the dress that she is putting on.

Draw some curvy lines to the end of the dress to make the dress come real. Do the same for the hat too.

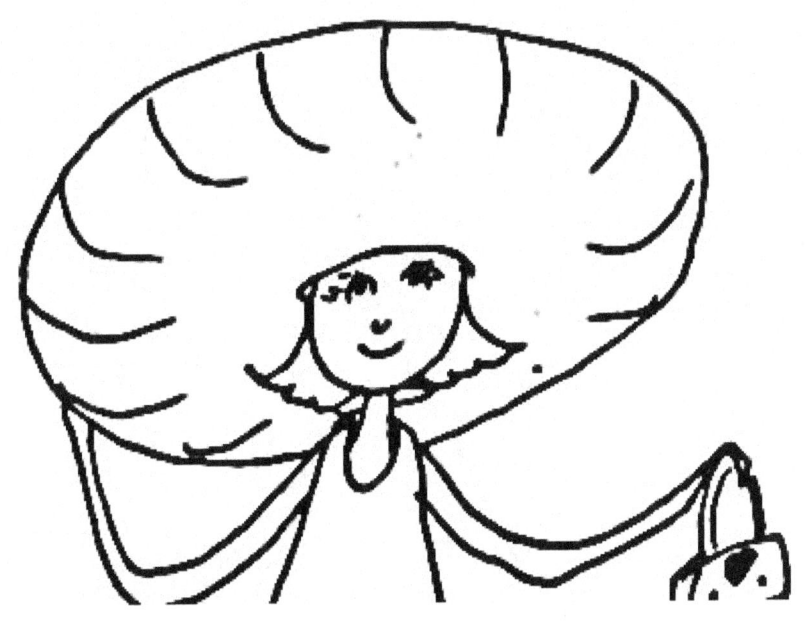

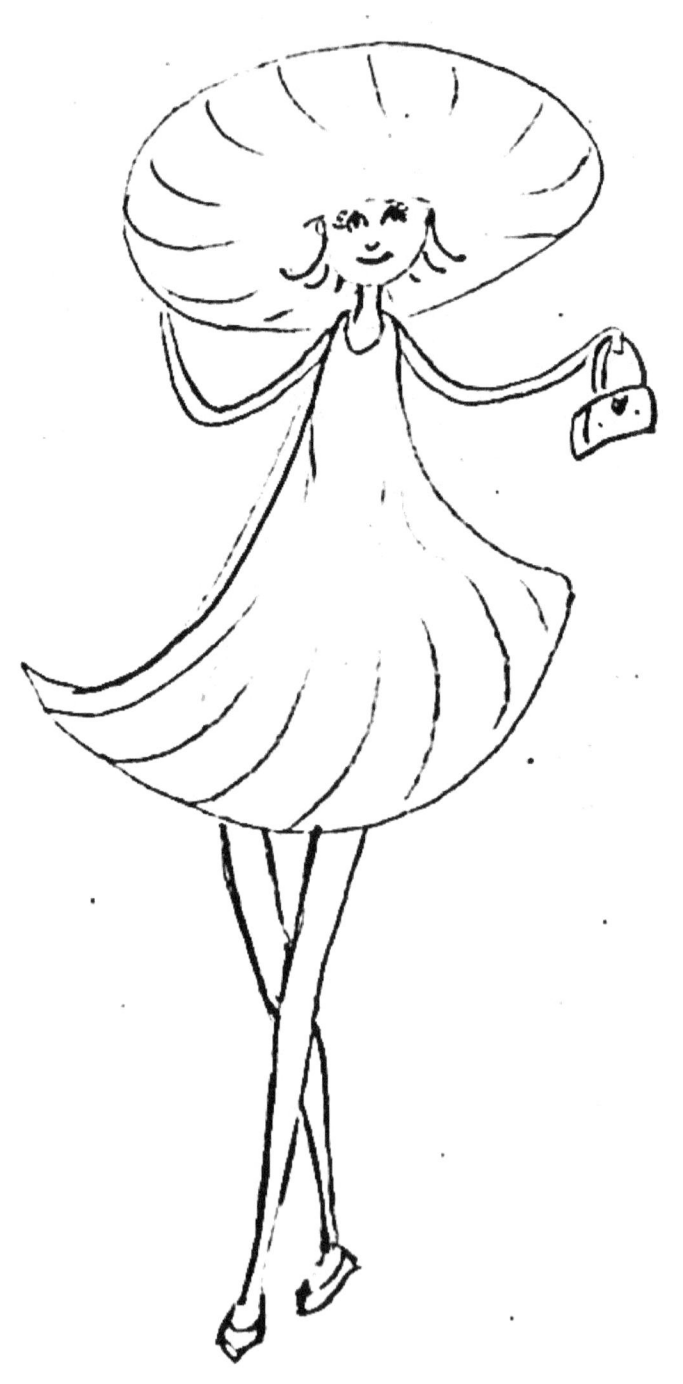

With the final diagram coming to life, proceed to erase some of the feature outlines that you will not need. Share her shoes darker or in any color that you want. Use a stronger pencil to make the outline of the body stand out, the outline of her hair, and the neckline for her dress. The final diagram should look like the one below.

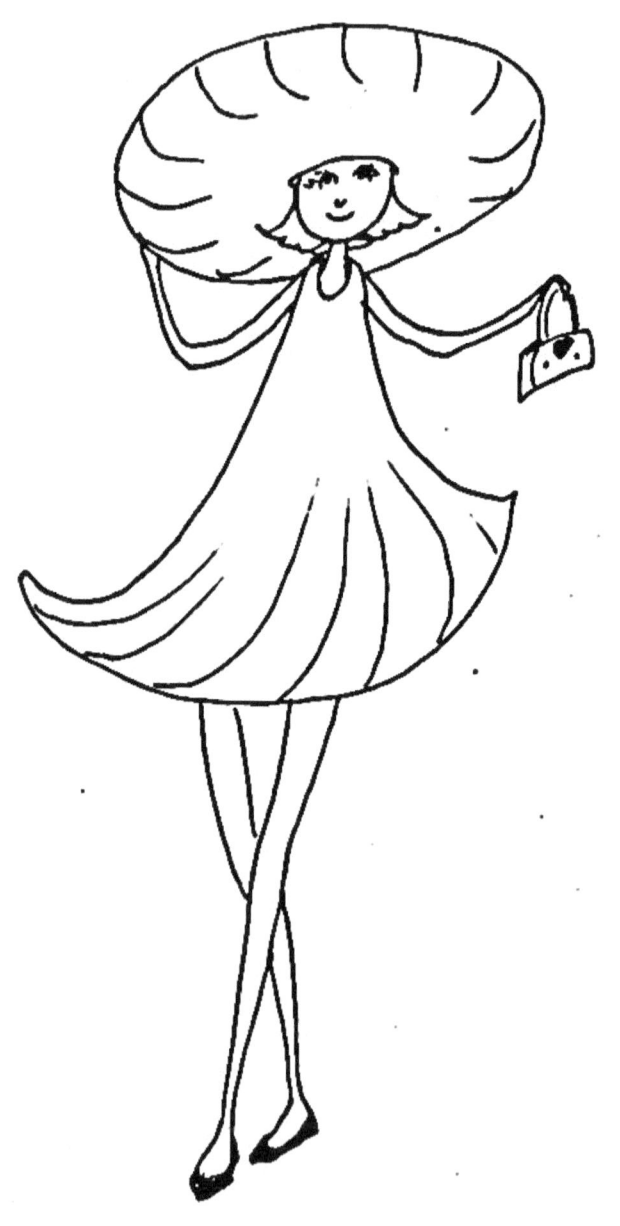

Chapter 3: Drawing a picture of a grown woman

So far we are making some good progress with some of the common drawings that you might have come to learn about. You should have already seen how easy it is to use simple lines and ellipses to draw nice pictures of grown human beings.

In this case we want to draw a picture of a grown woman. Could be someone's mom, aunt or teacher.

Start off with the basic outline. We will draw an oval shape for the head as shown below.

From the head, use two lines for the shoulders to show where we will have her neck. At the end of either of these lines, the outline for the arms and the upper body will form. This outline will be done with simple curved lines as shown.

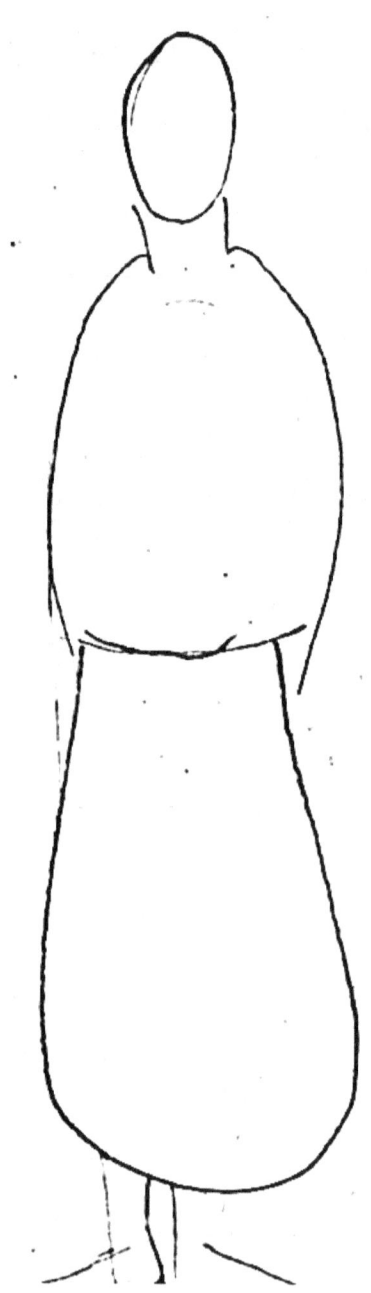

Draw an outline for her skirt and her legs as you can see in the diagram above. For the skirt, you will need some sense of continuity when you are drawing this, so start off from one side and continue to the other as shown.

For the legs, use simple lines to mark the outline as shown above.

This is a very simple diagram and the steps are easy to follow.

With the basic outline done, now we get back to the head and start making the features stand out. Start with the neckline. She appears to be putting on something that looks like a pull-neck. Use some simple lines to make that one stand out too.

Next up we will draw the outline of the arms from where we designed the outline for the top part of her body.

Use two lines within the larger curve you drew earlier to mark the position of her hands and at the same time to show the outline for the upper part of her body as shown below.

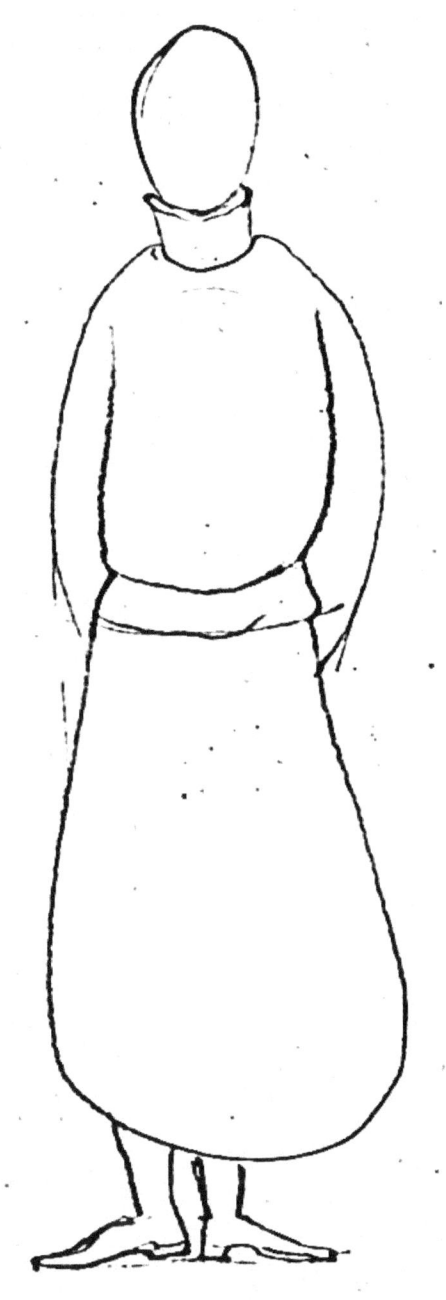

Add another line to her waistline to make it more prominent. This will also act as an outline for her skirt too.

Move lower to her legs and make her shoes and legs more prominent than they were in the earlier diagram.

Now let's move on to the finer details of her body.

Starting back from the head again, draw her yes, her nose and her lips. This you will do with really simple lines. You will also need to think of the hair. Use simple lines to make the outline of her hair stand out.

For the clothing that she is putting on around her neck, try and make it stand out by drawing some simple lines on it as shown below

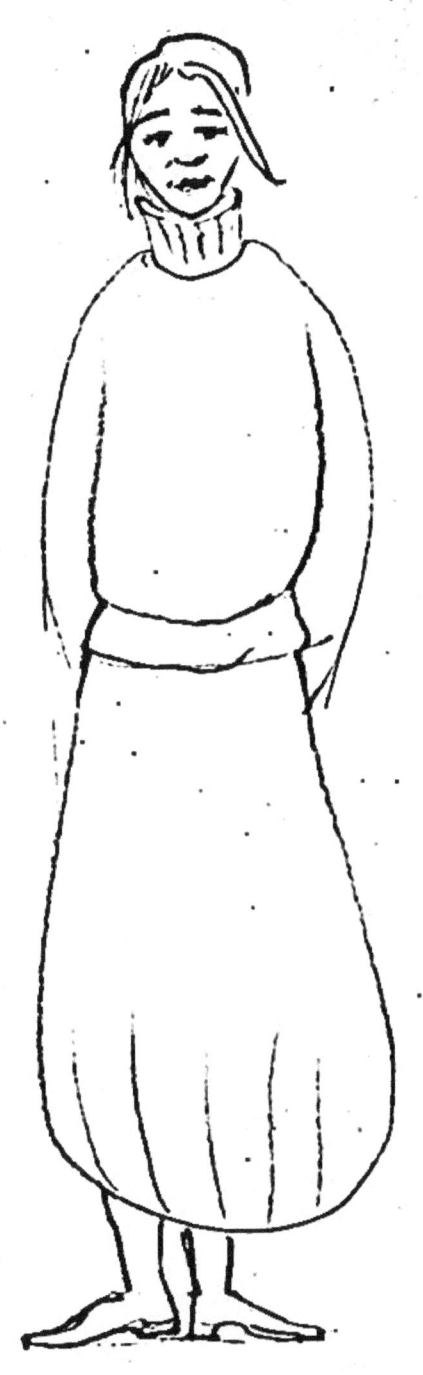

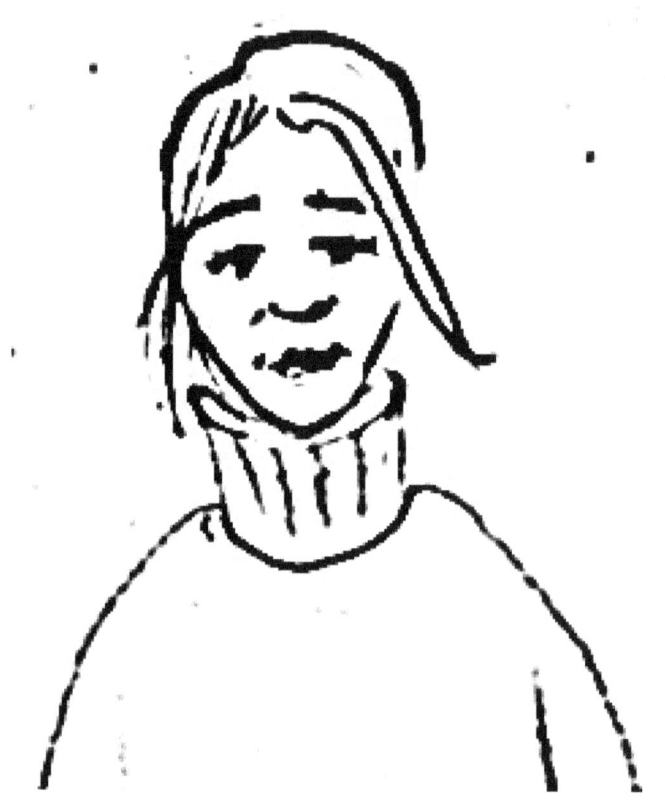

Next move to her skirt and use simple lines running from the bottom of her skirt upwards. These lines will disappear somewhere in the middle of her skirt.

You are now looking at the final outline of her body

To put some final touches on this diagram, first erase all the sections of this diagram that you do not need. After that, proceed to put an ornament around her neck. For this necklace, you will only need to use some really tiny circles and tiny joining lines.

Since the outline is now looking better, use a darker pencil to highlight the rest of her body and you will be good to go. Your final diagram should look like this

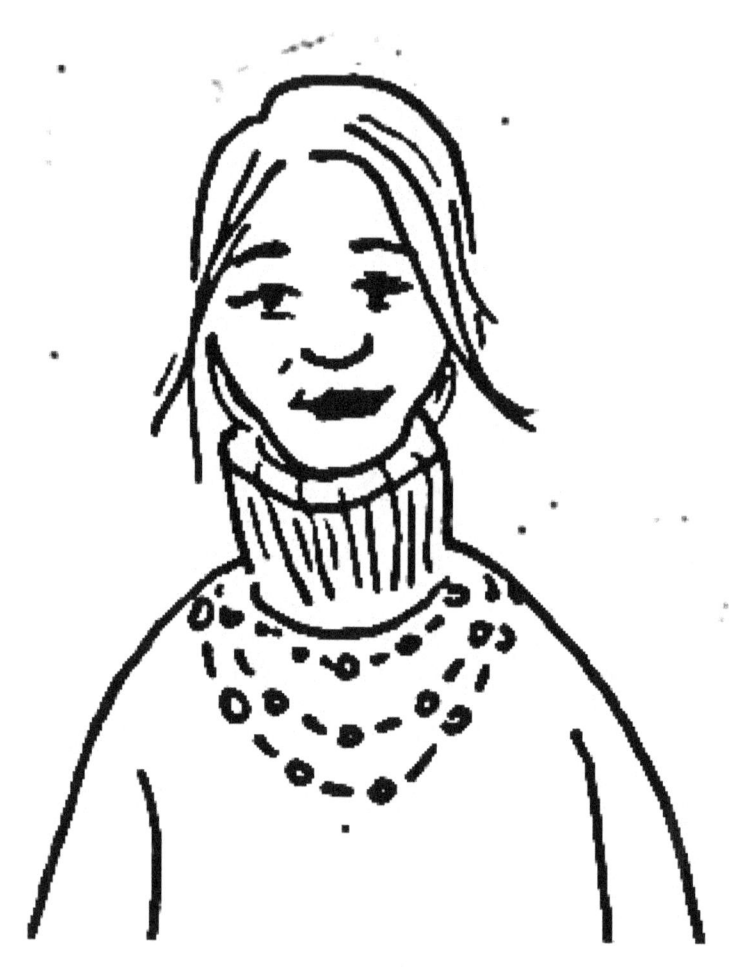

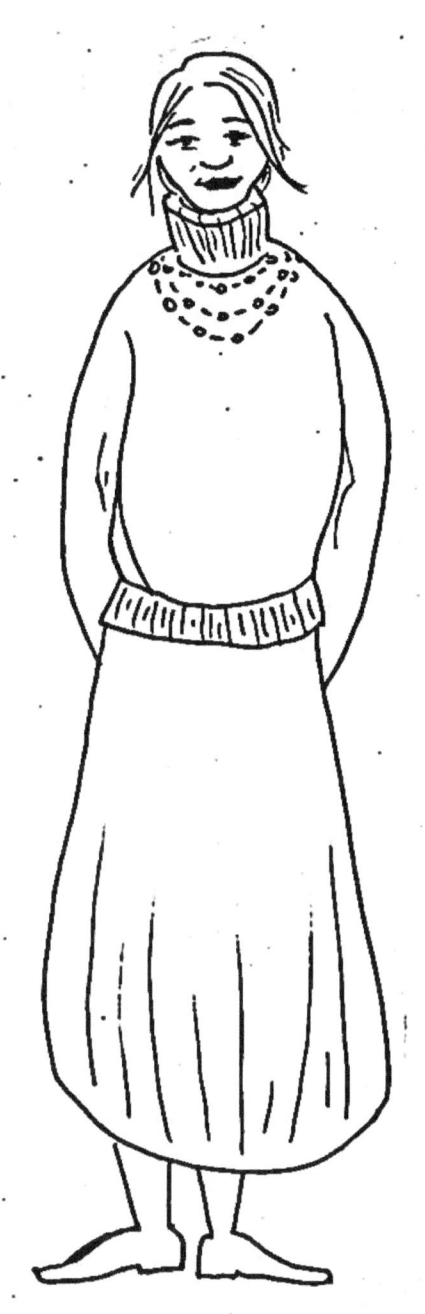

Chapter 4: Drawing a man with a suitcase

It is amazing how much work you can do with some of the simple shapes that you know about. Things like rectangles and oval shapes can really be useful to you in the long run, especially when you are trying to make sure that you can get one really awesome diagram done.

To start off this diagram, we will be drawing an outline for the hat and the rest of the body.

For the hat, an oval shape will do. Between the hat and the rest of the body, use two lines to connect these two parts. It is from these two lines that we will be able to get an outline for the head and the facial features.

Two rectangles can work for the upper part of the body. For these rectangles however, make sure that the lower part is narrower than the top part on both sides of the chest as shown below.

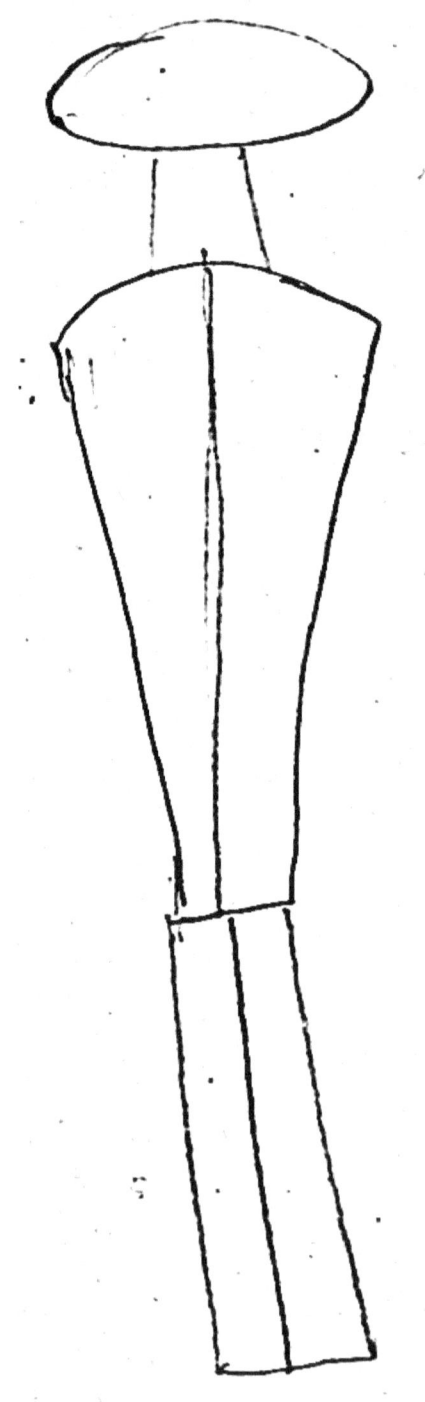

Starting off from the midsection of the body, draw another rectangle for the lower part of the body. This should be where we will have the legs and the shoes. Use a line in the middle to mark the section between two legs.

Next we will start bringing out the outlines for the body carefully. Starting off with the head, we will first make the outline for the top part of the hat as shown in the diagram below.

After that, move lower to the facial structure and outline the chin and the shape of the head as shown.

We will also try to carve out sections of the body, so that the outline of his coat can become prominent.

Start two lines from the neck area, meeting just a few centimeters off the chin. They should form something that looks like an inverted V.

Draw an outline for the pockets as shown.

Starting from the shoulder area, draw another outline for the arms. Once that is done, use two lines to show the protruding hand which will hold a briefcase. For the briefcase, just draw a rectangle as shown.

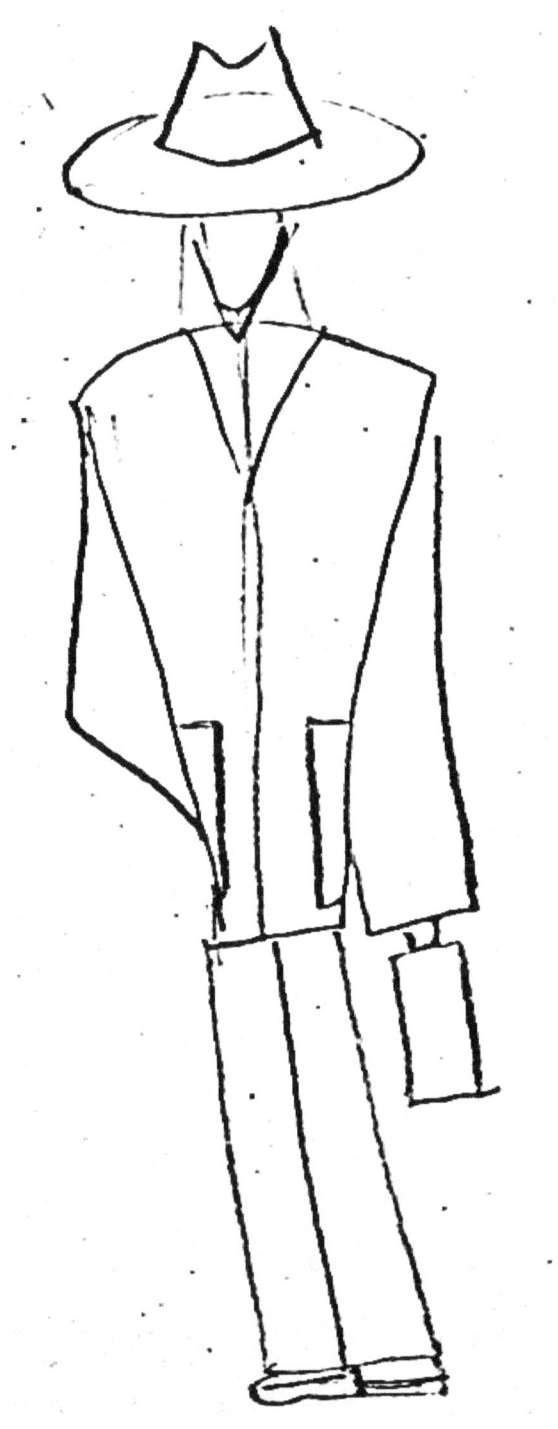

This makes your work a whole lot easier. Having done that, draw an outline for the shoes

With the figure of this man coming out clearly, we can now start putting the final touches to the body. Start from the head again. It is always good to start from the top so that you do not miss anything at all.

Trace out the outline for the hat and the face. Use darker lines to show the moustache for this guy. Draw the eyes and the nose as shown below.

Moving further down to the blazer, draw three small circles as shown to indicate the buttons for his blazer.

It appears he works for some corporation, so his blazer will have to have some sort of a badge for his workplace. Do that high up on the blazer, just slightly off the shoulder as shown below.

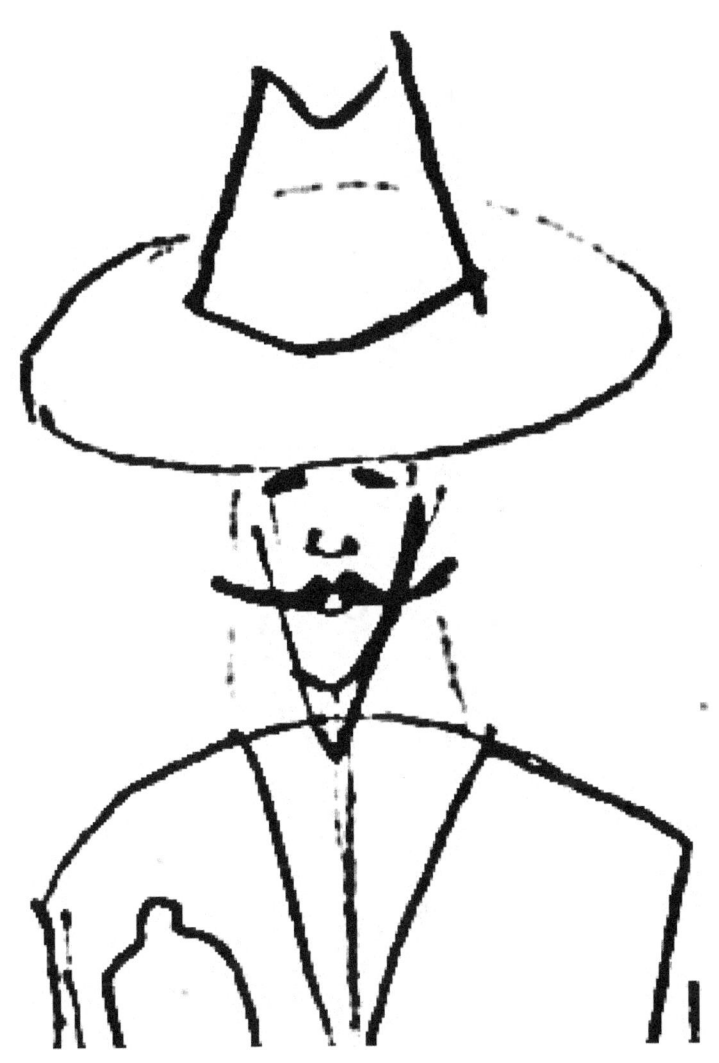

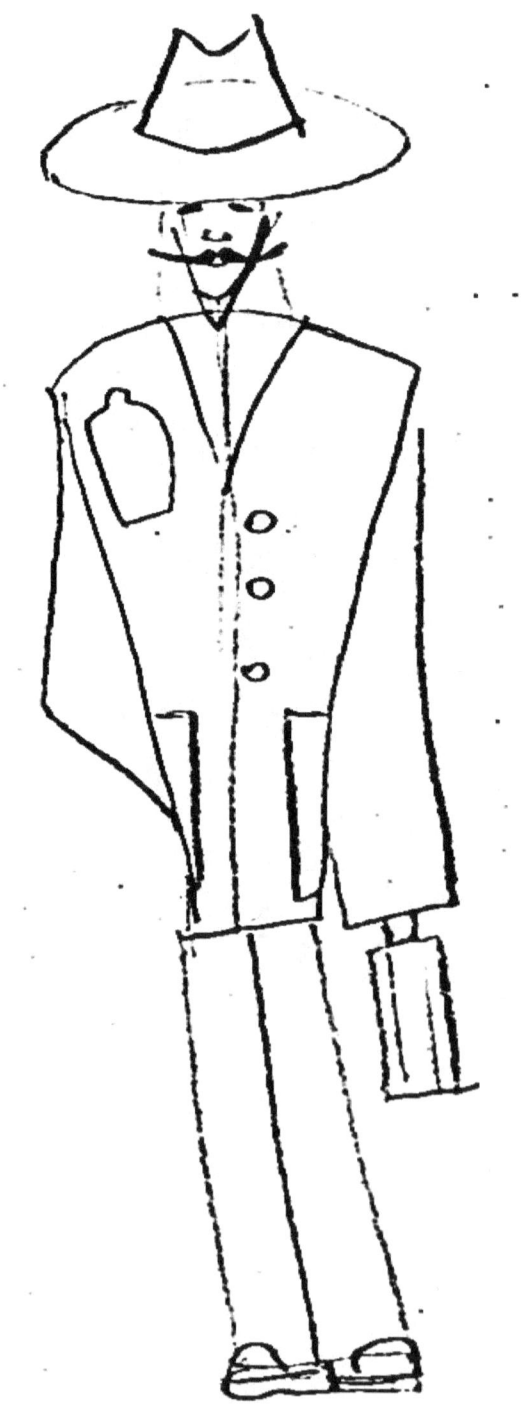

Use two lines to turn the briefcase from a mere rectangle to a real briefcase as shown above.

Since the final outline is coming alive, you can now use an eraser to get rid of all the other parts of the body that you might not need for this diagram. After that, everything else will be okay. Use a darker pen to make the body stand out.

Chapter 5: Drawing an old woman

We will now learn how to draw a picture of an old woman. To start you off, draw an oval shape that will be the outline for her head and her hat.

From the oval shape, use two curved lines to show the outline for the rest of her body as shown.

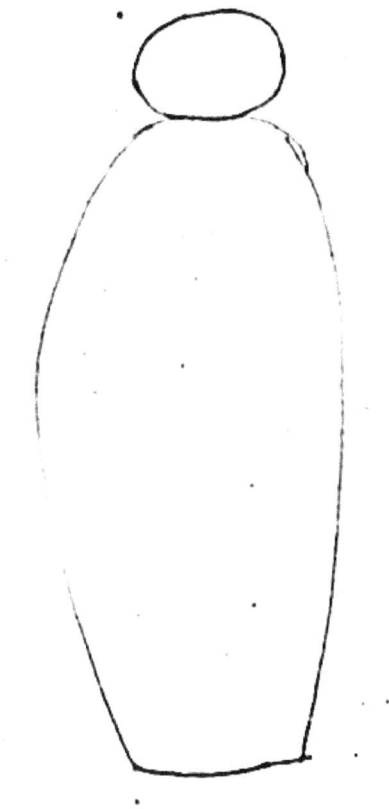

Go back to the head and draw a semicircular ring around the oval that outlines the head. This ring will indicate the outline for her hat.

Draw two lines on both sides of her upper body that will show an outline for her arms. Just underneath the outline for the arms, you will then draw a curved line that will be her waistline.

Just like that, you already have a very good outline for the body of this woman as shown below.

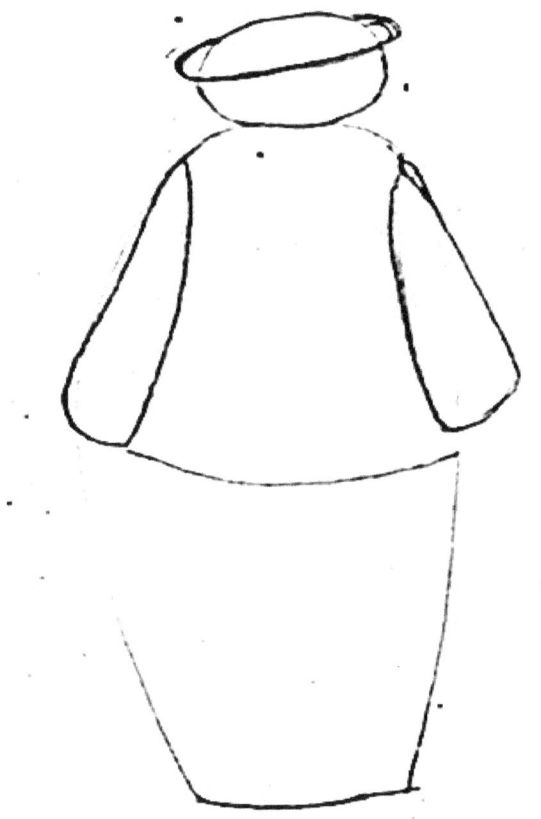

With the outline already done, we can now start adding the finer details to grandma. Start off from the head again.

On the outline that you drew for her head and the hat, take a darker pencil and make a bold shaded ring on her head. This will indicate the final form of her hat and head.

Let's move lower down to her shoulders. Use two curved liens to draw the outline for her half-coat. Between these two lines, you should also be able to draw another small curved line just underneath the chin. This will show us the outline for the blouse that she is putting on inside as shown below.

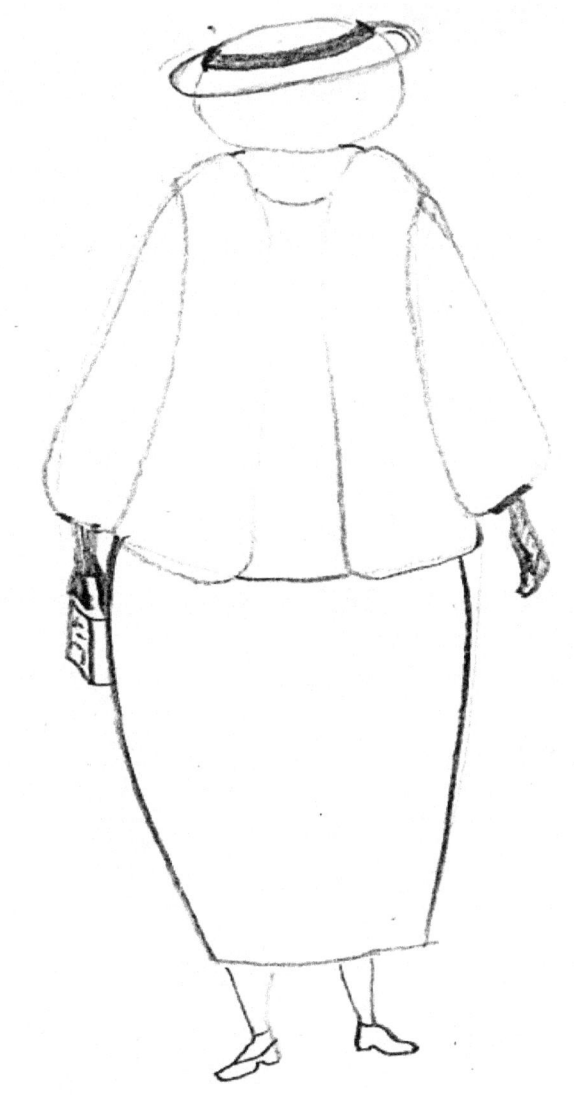

From the basic outline you can now draw her hands on both sides of her body as shown above. We will also give her a purse to carry as shown.

Moving lower, use simple lines to draw her legs. Do not try to be too creative, just use simple lines and you will be good to go. Other than that, do not also forget to draw the outline for her shoes as shown above.

We move back up to the head and erase the features of the earlier outline that we do not need. From there, we will then draw a good outline for the facial features. In this case, draw the eyes, the nose and the lips. Do not forget to design the grandma frown. For this you will use two lines from her nose, slanting in opposite directions.

Our outline for grandma is almost complete, and you should have the following picture.

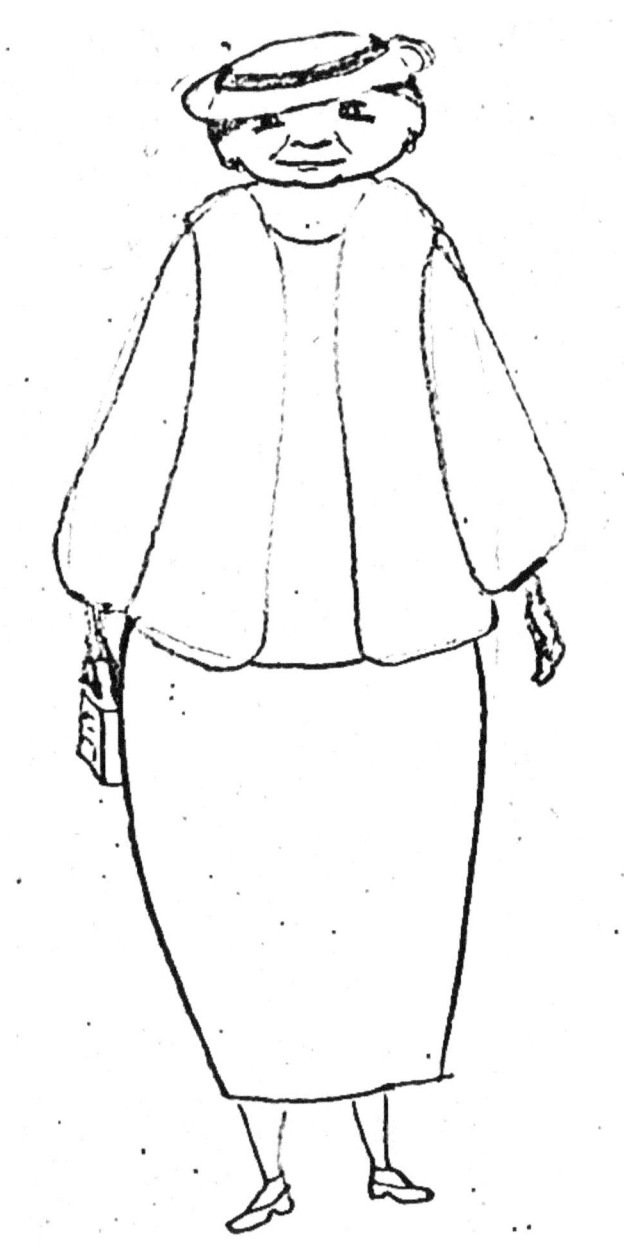

With this part of the diagram done, you are now ready to make the rest of the outline become final. To finalize the diagram, start off from the head once again. You will use simple lines to make the outline of her eyes become real and look more mature for her age.

After that, go lower to the neck area. Draw two curves on either side of her neck to form wrinkles.

Decorate the old lady's coat as shown. Use small dots to indicate the buttons, and small lines to indicate the button holes. Shade her arms dark or black, whichever appeals to you.

Go lower to her legs and make her shoes darker.

The final picture that you should have should look like this.

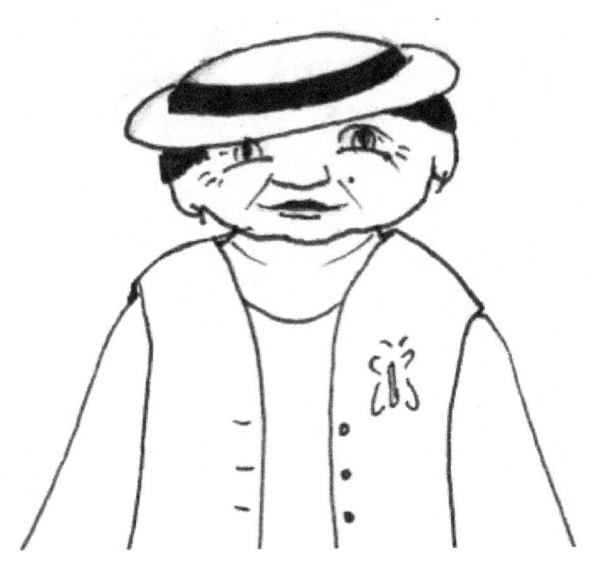

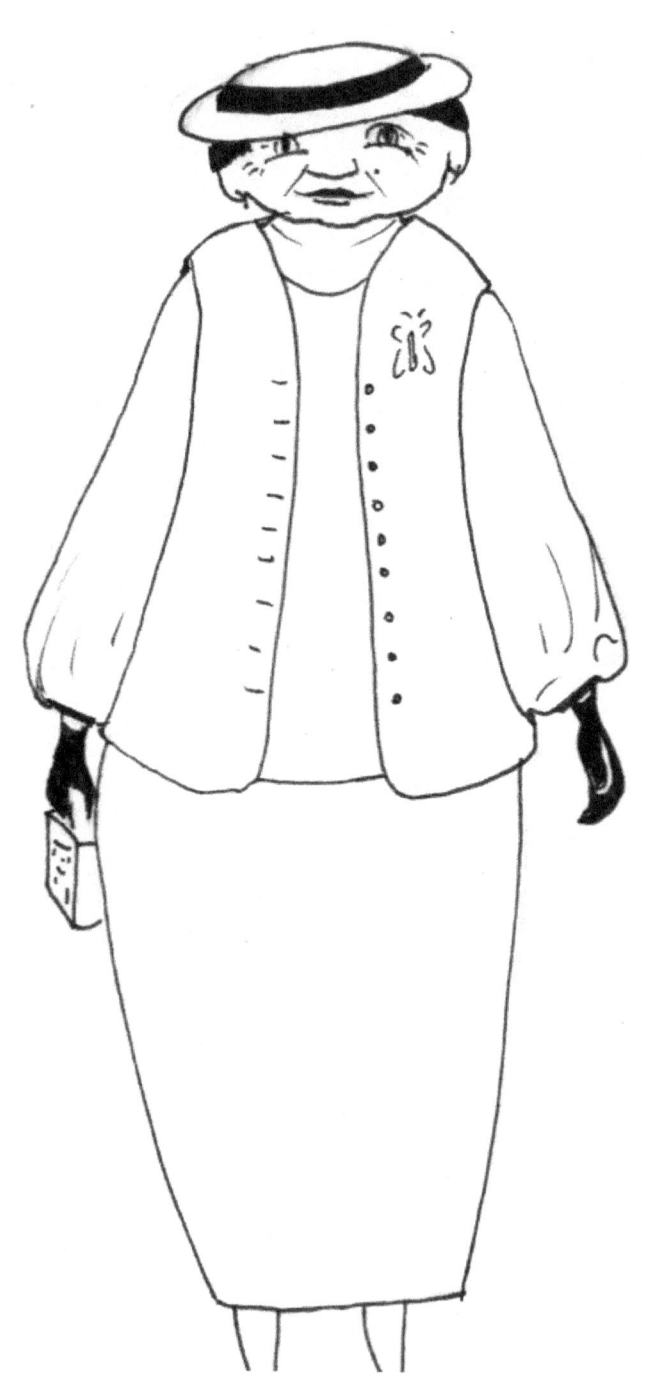

Chapter 6: Drawing a picture of an old man

We will use the same concepts that we used before to draw the old man in this picture. Once again, basic shapes and ellipses will come in handy for you. To start off, draw an oval shape for the head. This shape will however have a slight difference in the structure. It will have a sharp edge at the lower end, looking like a corner of a triangle.

Just under halfway from the middle of the head, draw a rectangular ellipse as shown. The top end of this shape is supposed to be wider than the lower end. This will form the chest of the man.

At the end of this, you will then draw two lines from either side of the lower end of the rectangle. These two are supposed to give us the outline for the legs of this man. Once you are don with that, go on and draw an outline for the shoes.

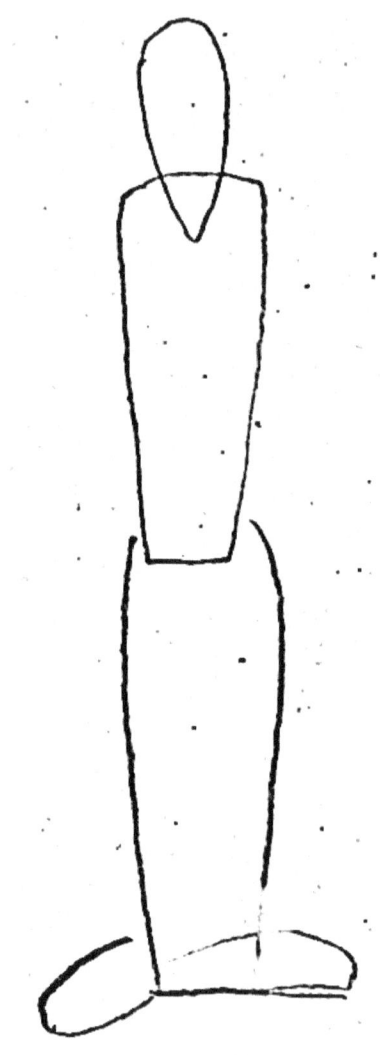

From this basic outline, everything else that you would love to draw about this man should be easier now. We can then more from here one step at a time until we have the final diagram of the man we want to draw.

The old man that we will be drawing is supposed to be carrying two small cans/buckets on either side of a bent stick/rod. For this reason, we will have to make sure that we do all we can to make this outline too.

Following on from the outline that you had earlier, draw two curved lines from either side of the man's shoulders. These should be indicative of the stick from where the buckets will hang.

We then move to the neckline. The neckline for this man will follow through from the sharp edge that we drew from the outline of the head. Draw a cure around that sharp edge (which should indicate the chin), moving from one side of the shoulder to the other as shown.

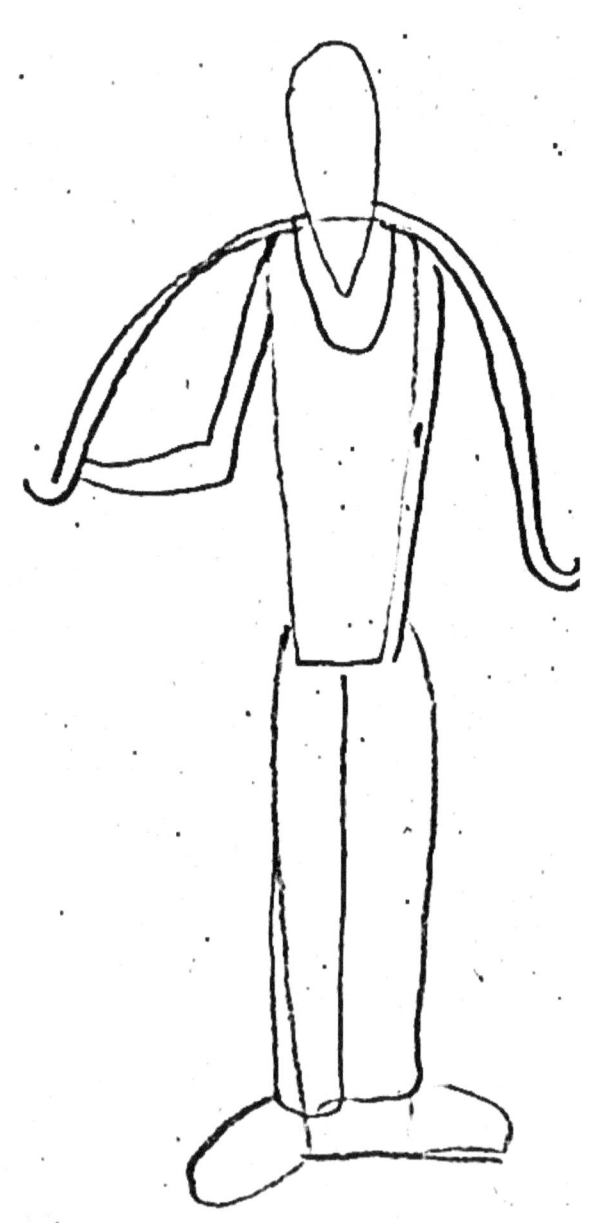

Use two simple lines again to draw an outline for his right arm. After that move to the lower section of the body and draw a line in between, a line that will separate the two legs.

Having done that, go on and start an outline for the shoes as shown above.

The outline is coming through finally. Now we will start working on the finer details.

As we have always done, we start from the head downwards. So, starting from the head, we will draw an outline for the nose. Together with this, we will also put some shades on either side to make an outline for the moustache.

Remember the sharp edge of the head that was supposed to be the chin? Well, shade it with light lines, running from the edges of the moustache that you just drew.

Therefore we have managed to give him a moustache and a beard as shown.

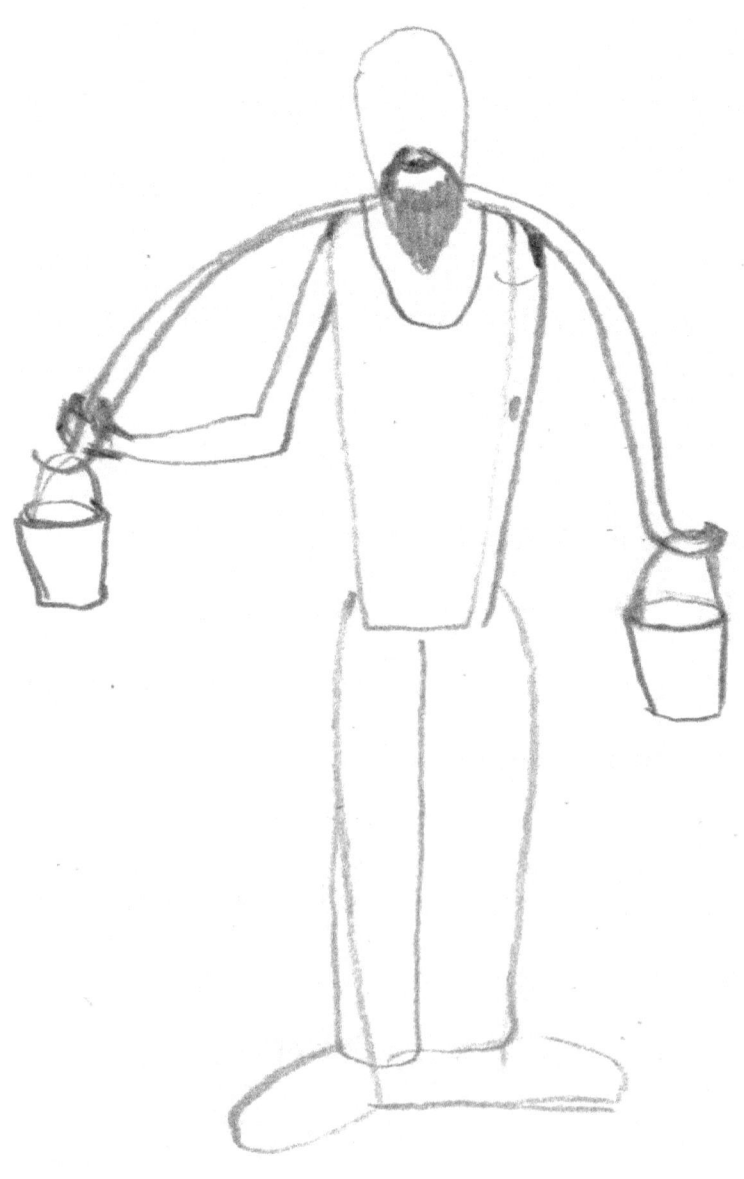

Next we will draw the outline for his other arm, which appears to be pocketing as shown above. On either ends of the stick that he is supporting on his back, draw two small buckets.

We then go back to the head again, use dark shades further up his head to show the receding hairline. Apart from that we will also draw the eyebrows as shown below.

Draw a curve from one side of his shoulder to the other. This will form the outline for his vest. On this vest outline, shade interchanging stripes of grey.

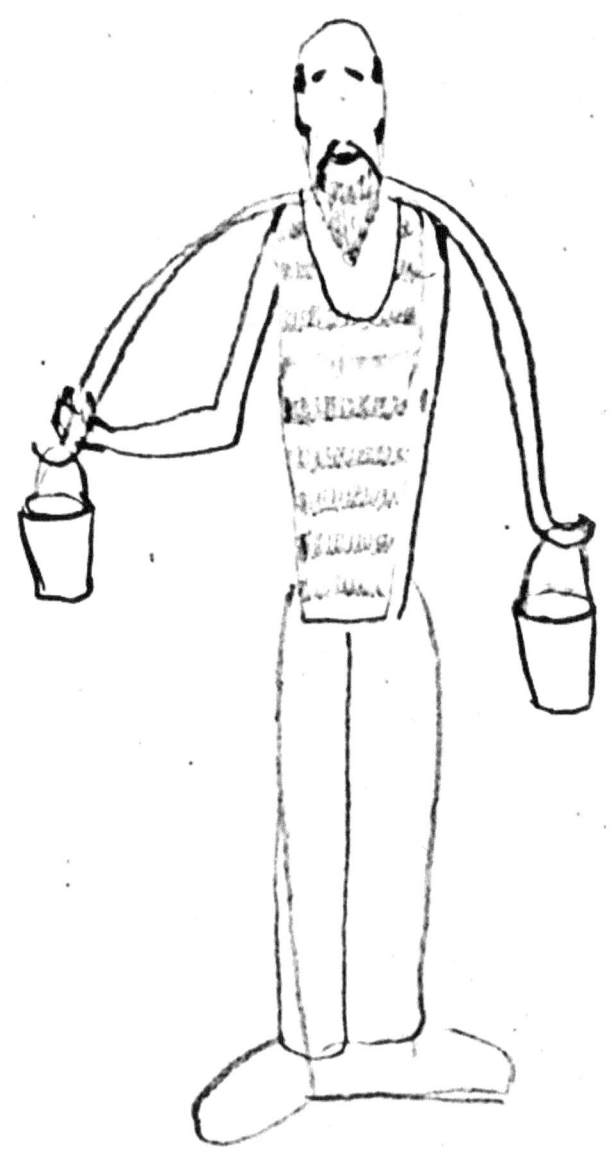

The outline for the old man is finally looking real, so you can now focus on shading it, make the grey shades darker.

Draw the rest of the facial features; the eyes, the nose and the lips.

Use small lines and dots as shown to show the pockets, then move down to his shoes and use simple lines to make the pattern shown below. Your final figure should look like this.

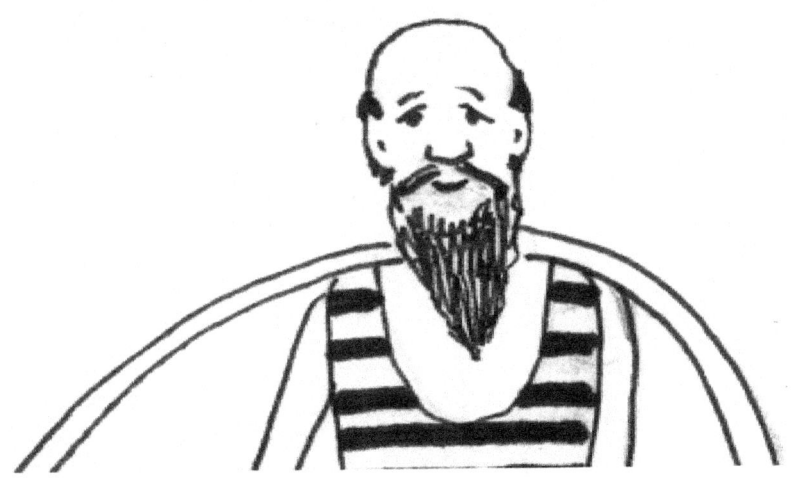

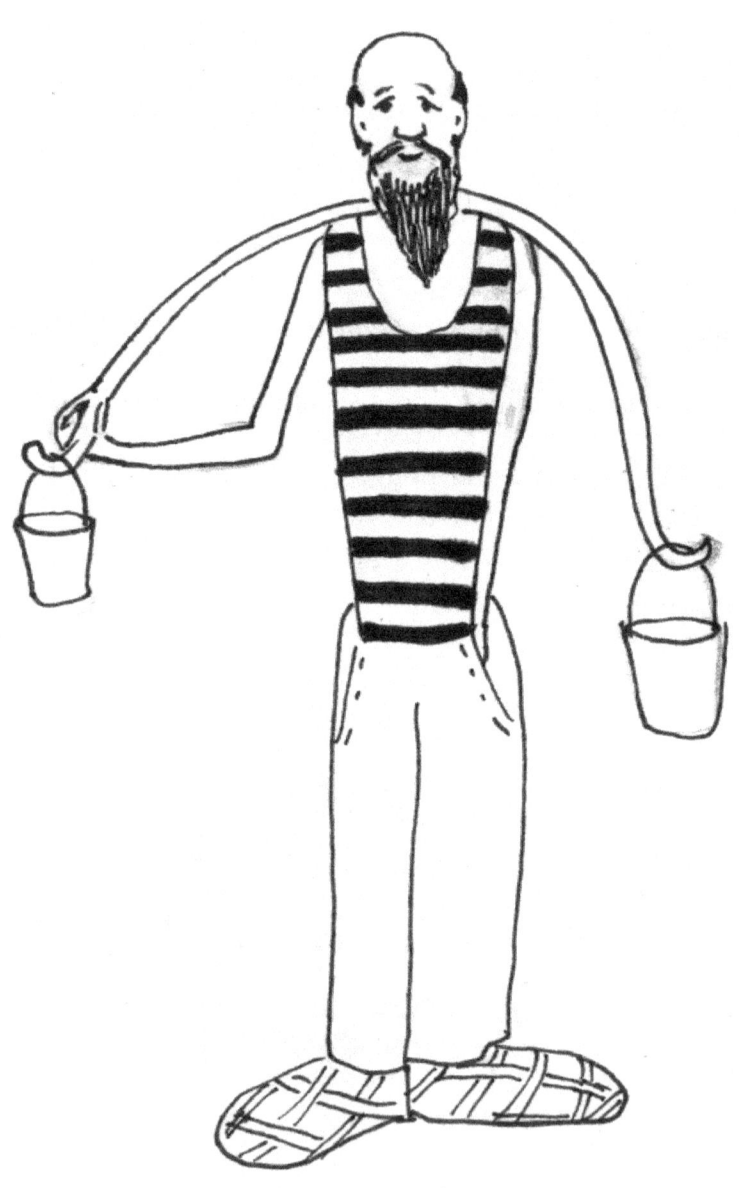

Conclusion

From the work that we have done herein, there is nothing that should make your work harder, or stand in your way if you want to learn how to draw human forms. You can start off easy, work your way up one human character at a time.

In the long run, this will become an activity that you will definitely come to enjoy. Over the years we have seen lots of individuals come to learn how to make the best use of such skill, and you too can do it.

For those who are interested in art, this will be a really good way to start off, build things one step at a time as you come to appreciate the best there is to artistry. You can also build on such skills and become a better artist over time.

Do not just limit your skills to the human forms that we have in here. There are so many other forms that you can exercise with. Remember that the ultimate goal here is to have fun while learning to draw some of the easiest human forms you have ever come across so far.

Thank you!

Thank you for choosing our book, we hope you found it interesting and helpful.

If you liked the book, please give us a favor to write your review.

We would really appreciate this!

If you would like to have a bonus – **FREE BOOK**, please send the screenshot of your review to this e-mail:

kelly.artbooks@gmail.com and we will send you a **FREE BOOK** in PDF as a **GIFT!****

Hope to see you in our future books and good luck in your drawing experience!

** in the e-mail subject please mention the name of the book you reviewed and the author.

www.ingramcontent.com/pod-product-compliance
Lightning Source LLC
Chambersburg PA
CBHW071622170526
45166CB00003B/1155

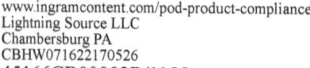